Contents

Some words are shown in bold, **like this**. You can find out what they mean by looking in the glossary.

LET'S LOOK AT

British trees!

Trees are an important part of our world. You can see them almost anywhere, from peaceful **forests** to people's gardens! Read on to find out about all the different places where trees grow in the United Kingdom.

PINEWOODS

Pinewoods are forests of **pine** trees, such as the Scots pine. They mainly grow in the mountains and hills of Scotland. They are an important habitat for rare animals, such as red squirrels, and rare birds, such as the capercaillie.

ANCIENT WOODLAND

Ancient means very old. The trees in ancient woodland have been growing for many hundreds of years – since about 1600 in England and Wales, and 1750 in Scotland. In spring, a carpet of bluebells often covers the forest floor. Lots of animals, from tawny owls to badgers, make their homes in ancient woodland.

WET WOODLAND

The trees in wet woodland grow next to water. Birch and willow trees love the damp soil near rivers, streams and marshes.

LOWLAND WOODS

Lowland woods grow in low-lying countryside. The trees here are mostly **deciduous** (they lose their leaves in autumn).

What do trees need to grow?

Trees are the biggest living things on Earth. They need plenty of room to grow.

With enough room, they can get the other things they need to survive:

- light
- **nutrients** from the soil
- water
- **carbon dioxide**. Carbon dioxide is a gas in the air. Just as people need **oxygen** from the air to survive, trees need carbon dioxide. They absorb carbon dioxide through their leaves, branches and **bark**. Trees make their own food by combining carbon dioxide, water and energy from the Sun. This is called **photosynthesis**.

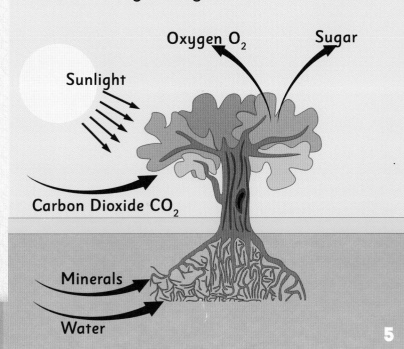

Oxygen O_2

Sugar

Sunlight

Carbon Dioxide CO_2

Minerals

Water

ORCHARDS

Orchards are special areas planted with fruit trees, such as apple, pear and cherry. Orchards do not grow naturally. The trees are planted by fruit-farmers. The farmers care for them. They gather the fruit when it is ripe and ready to harvest.

GARDENS

Trees also grow in many people's gardens. They attract wildlife, such as insects and small mammals, to the garden. Birds nest among the branches in garden trees and **shrubs**.

PARKS

Parks are open, green spaces in towns and cities. Most of the trees in parks were planted by people. These include elm trees. Sadly, Dutch elm disease has killed hundreds of elm trees in Britain. Many elms have been cut down to stop the disease spreading.

TOWNS AND CITIES

Trees that grow in towns and cities are an important habitat for the animals that live among us, like bats and birds. But these trees can cause problems if they grow too big. **Tree surgeons** cut and trim the branches to make the trees safe.

What is a habitat?

A habitat is the place in nature where an animal, plant or tree lives. Britain has many different habitats. Trees grow in the habitat that best suits them. The Douglas fir needs lots of water to survive. It grows in areas where it rains a lot.

Trees themselves can also provide habitats for animals and minibeasts. See pages 26–27 for more information about the creatures that make trees their home.

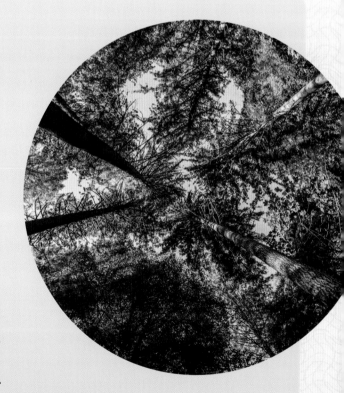

Parts of a tree

From the deepest roots to the highest branch, every single part of a tree has a special job to do.

FLOWERS

The flowers that grow on trees may look pretty, but they also have an important job to do. For new trees to grow, the **pollen** inside one tree's flowers needs to be moved to another tree's flowers. Insects, birds and the wind carry pollen between flowers. This means the tree can make **seeds**. The seeds grow into new trees.

BRANCHES

Leaves, flowers and fruit grow along branches.

TRUNK

The trunk supports the rest of the tree. It gives a tree its shape. It carries water and **nutrients** from the roots up to the crown.

CROWN

The crown is all the leaves and branches at the top of the tree. It provides shade for the roots. It also collects the Sun's energy to help the tree grow.

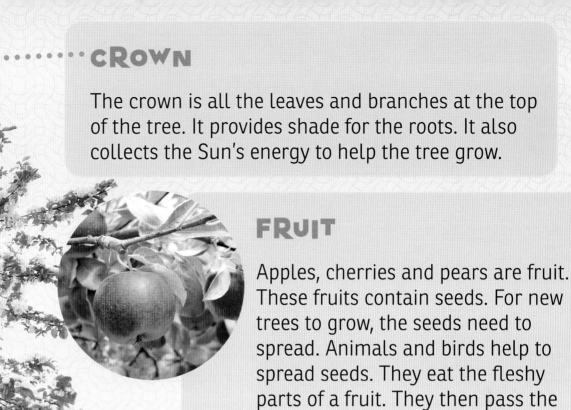

FRUIT

Apples, cherries and pears are fruit. These fruits contain seeds. For new trees to grow, the seeds need to spread. Animals and birds help to spread seeds. They eat the fleshy parts of a fruit. They then pass the hard seeds in their droppings.

LEAVES

Leaves come in many different shapes and sizes. They are the "food factory" of a tree. They take in **carbon dioxide** and energy from the Sun. They use them to turn water and nutrients from the soil into food for the tree.

ROOTS

Roots are the part of the tree that grow underground. They collect water and nutrients from the soil. Roots also hold the tree in place and stop it from tipping over.

Parts of a forest

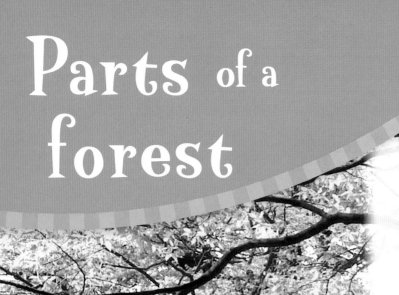

Forests are important habitats for thousands of different mammals, birds and insects.

UNDERSTORY

The understory is the layer beneath the canopy. Not much light reaches here. Only those plants, **shrubs** and bushes that like shade can grow here, such as rhododendrum and hawthorn. Deer nibble at the shrubs.

rhododendrum   hawthorn   roe deer

FOREST FLOOR

The forest floor is the bottom layer. Very little light reaches the forest floor. Here you will find tree **seedlings**, rotten wood, leaves and **pine** needles. Minibeasts, such as earthworms and woodlice, feed on the rotting plants and logs. Ivy, grass and moss also grow here.

moss   woodlouse   mouse

CANOPY

The canopy is the "roof" of the forest. Here you'll find the crowns (branches, twigs and leaves) of the largest trees in the forest, such as oak, ash and beech. The tallest trees get the most sunlight. Large birds, like buzzards, build their nests in the big, strong branches.

oak tree

buzzard

FIELD LAYER

The field layer is the layer just above the ground. Woodland flowers, such as primrose, and ferns, like bracken, grow here in spring before the canopy layer grows its leaves and blocks the sunlight. Butterflies fly between the flowers, feeding on the flower **pollen**.

primrose

butterfly

fern

Deciduous trees

OAK

acorn

Have you ever noticed that some trees lose their leaves for some of the year, while others do not? Trees that lose their leaves are called **deciduous**. The trees that do not lose their leaves are **evergreen**.

The oak is Britain's most common deciduous tree. Oak trees are massive, sturdy giants when fully grown. But they start life as a tiny acorn!

Deciduous trees begin to lose their leaves in autumn. First, the leaves change colour, from light green to bright orange. Finally, they turn red-brown just before they drop.

Like some animals, deciduous trees "hibernate" during winter. This means they go to sleep, or stop growing. This is called being dormant. This helps trees to save energy and stay alive during the cold winter.

ELM

Elms grow in damp soil near water. The English elm has greenish flowers and red fruits. Their **seeds** are light and papery. The wind spreads the seeds far and wide.

WILLOW

Willow trees, like the weeping willow, grow near rivers and streams. They have long, soft flowers called catkins. Catkins get their name because they look and feel a bit like a cat's tail!

catkin

BEECH

common beech

Beech tree leaves are usually a lime green colour. They have wavy edges and a pointed tip. But the copper beech has dark purple leaves!

copper beech

HAWTHORN

Hawthorn trees are covered in tiny white flowers in the spring. They are sometimes called May trees after the month in which they flower. Birds eat the bright red berries in the autumn.

BIRCH

Birch trees are tall and thin. The silver birch's **bark** looks different to other trees. It is silvery-white and thin, a bit like tissue paper.

ROWAN

Rowan trees are sometimes called mountain ash trees. This is because they mainly grow high up on mountains. The rowan's leaves look a bit like feathers.

PLANE

Plane trees, such as the London plane, are a common sight on city streets. The flaky bark is grey, olive and cream in colour. It looks a lot like camouflage! The plane tree's fruits grow in strings of small, round balls.

HORSE CHESTNUT

horse chestnut flower

Horse chestnut trees can grow to a height of 40 metres. They can live for 300 years. They grow mainly in parks and on village greens, rather than in **forests**. You can easily recognize this tree by its conkers in the autumn.

SYCAMORE

Sycamore trees have broad, five-fingered leaves. The **seeds** that are produced in the autumn have wings. They spin around as they fall to the ground. Some people call them helicopters!

helicopter seeds

What is a conker?

A conker is the hard, brown, round seed of a horse chestnut tree. It is protected by a hard, spiky case. Conkers drop to the ground in autumn. The hard case cracks open and the seed sends out a shoot. Soon the shoot will grow into a horse chestnut tree.

FIELD MAPLE

There are many types of maple trees. The field maple is the only type that is native to the UK. They have yellow flowers. Their **seeds** are similar to sycamore seeds (see page 15). They often grow in hedgerows beside fields. Aphids like to live on maple trees. So do ladybirds and birds, which eat the aphids. The **sap** the trees produce can be used to make syrup for us to eat.

HAZEL

hazelnuts

Hazel trees flower early in spring, before their soft, hairy leaves appear. Their flowers are long catkins. In autumn, hazelnuts grow in little clusters. Animals like to eat the nuts, including dormice, squirrels, woodpeckers and other birds. Long ago, hazel trees were believed to have magical powers.

COMMON LIME

Lime trees are the tallest **deciduous** trees in the UK. You can see them growing in streets or parks in towns. They have delicate leaves, shaped like hearts. Their sweet-smelling flowers can be used to make tea!

SWEET CHESTNUT

Sweet chestnut trees have long, slim leaves with a jagged edge. The nuts appear in autumn. People like to eat sweet chestnuts. In the UK, we mostly get sweet chestnuts for eating from other countries. This is because summers here are not warm enough to make our chestnuts sweet.

ASH

Many types of moths like to lay their eggs on the leaves of ash trees. The caterpillars that hatch then eat the leaves. Ash trees can live for up to 400 years! Unfortunately, many die from a disease called 'ash dieback' before they reach old age.

ALDER

Alder trees produce catkins. But the catkins don't disappear after spring. Instead, they turn into brown, hard cones and stay on the tree through the winter. Alders do not lose their leaves as early as most other deciduous trees. They stay green well into autumn.

alder cones

Evergreen trees

What is a conifer?

Trees that keep their leaves all year round are called **evergreen**. Since evergreen trees do not shed all their leaves in one go, they stay green all year round.

Many evergreen trees have needles. These are very thin, sharp leaves. Needles are longest on **pine** trees. They are prickliest on spruce trees! Most evergreen trees shed a small number of old needles every few years. New needles grow in their place. This means the trees never look bare.

A conifer is a type of tree. Most conifers have **cones**. Cones are the **seeds**. Conifers also have needles or scales rather than flat leaves. Most conifers are evergreen. There are three main types of British conifer: the Scots pine, the juniper and the yew.

PINE

The Scots pine is the largest of Britain's conifers. It grows mainly in pinewood **forests** in Scotland. It has a reddish-brown trunk and big green or grey cones.

YEW

Yews have small, straight needles. Their seeds are inside bright red coats. Blackbirds love to eat these seeds. The branches are packed tightly together, which makes the yew tree a great place for small birds to nest in. You can often see yew trees in churchyards.

pine cones

JUNIPER

The needles of juniper trees are green on top and silvery-grey underneath. The juniper tree grows bunches of purple-blue berries. Juniper berries are used to add flavour to drinks and sauces.

CEDAR

Cedar trees were brought to the UK in the 1700s to be planted in the gardens of **stately homes**. Now you can usually find them in gardens or parks. They can survive well up mountains in other countries.

Is a cone a seed?

Cones are woody growths on **evergreen** trees. **Seeds** form inside the cones. The cone's scales open up to release the seeds. Animals or the wind carry the seeds to a new place. There they will grow into a new tree.

NORWAY SPRUCE

Queen Victoria and her husband, Prince Albert, made it fashionable to decorate a Norway spruce at Christmas. Now many people bring these trees into their homes over the festive period. The tree is also grown in **forests** for **timber**.

HOLLY

Holly trees are easy to spot. They have dark green, prickly leaves and bright red berries in winter. People decorate their homes with sprigs of holly at Christmas time.

Box

Box trees come in all shapes and sizes. Their branches are covered in waxy oval leaves. Gardeners trim the leaves and branches into any shape they like, from chickens to chess pieces!

HEATH

Heaths are a large family of trees and **shrubs** (like small trees). Rhododendrons are part of this family. They have shiny, dark green leaves. The leaves stay green all year round. In summer the shrub is covered in big white, pink or purple flowers.

What age do trees live to?

Trees live to different ages. Big trees, such as oaks and yews, can live for hundreds, sometimes even thousands of years. The Fortingall Yew in Scotland is thought to be the oldest tree in Britain. Some experts say it is 5,000 years old. That's older than Stonehenge, which was built in 2,500 BC!

If a tree is cut down, you can tell how old it was by counting the rings in its trunk. Each ring represents a year of the tree's life.

tree rings

Fruit trees

Fruit trees are a special type of tree. Some of our favourite fruits and nuts grow on these trees. Many gardeners grow fruit trees in their gardens or greenhouses. Farmers grow hundreds of these trees in **orchards**. Most fruit trees have come from other countries. They are not native to Britain. Read on to find out some fruit trees that grow well in Britain.

APPLE

There are thousands of different types of apples. The two main types are dessert apples and cooking apples. Common dessert apples grown here in Britain are cox, russet and braeburn. Apples taste delicious straight from the tree in the autumn.

CHERRY

Some cherry trees grow wild in the UK. However, the cherries we eat usually come from sweet cherry trees, grown on farms. Cherry trees have a mass of white or pink flowers in the spring.

PEAR

Pear trees have spiny branches. In spring they are covered in small white flowers. Blackbirds and thrushes like to feast on the fruits.

WALNUT

Walnut trees can grow very tall – up to 35 metres. Once pollinated, the flowers develop into a brown, wrinkled walnut inside a green, fleshy **husk**.

Life cycle of a fruit tree

All trees start out life as tiny **seeds**. From there they grow into tall trees.

Seeds: Seeds are the tiny, hard parts inside the apple. If they fall on the ground, they sprout roots and shoots. Slowly, they grow into a sapling (young tree) and eventually an adult tree. Then the life cycle starts again.

Adult tree

TREE LIFE CYCLE

Fruit: In autumn, the apples grow big. Some fall to the ground. Some are picked.

Once pollinated, the flowers begin to die. Fruit begins to develop.

Flowers: In spring the tree produces flowers. Inside the flower is pollen. Insects carry the **pollen** from flower to flower and to flowers on other trees. This is called **pollination**.

Unusual trees

Some of the trees in this book did not grow naturally in the UK. They were brought here for people to grow in gardens and parks. Now we are used to seeing some of these more unusual trees in this country.

EUROPEAN FAN PALM

This small palm tree has stiff, fan-shaped leaves. It also prefers hot summers. In Britain, gardeners wrap the tree's trunk in a thick material called burlap during winter. This helps the tree to survive the cold.

Countries: Italy, Portugal, Spain

COAST REDWOOD

This tree grows taller than any other on Earth. The tallest redwood in the United States is an amazing 115.7 metres tall. You would think that this means redwoods have large **cones**, but they are actually tiny! The trees also have a soft, red **bark**.

Country: USA

EUCALYPTUS

Eucalyptus trees are also called gum trees. There are over 700 types of eucalyptus. Their leaves make a strong-smelling oil. We use the oil to add flavour to cough sweets, perfume and toothpaste.

Country: Australia

GOLDEN LARCH

The golden larch is a pretty tree. People plant them in parks and gardens. In autumn, its needles turn bright gold-yellow. This is what gives the tree its name.

Country: China

JAPANESE MAPLE

Japanese maples are also called acers. They are small, **deciduous** trees. They are slow to grow and never get very tall. Their star-shaped leaves turn a beautiful deep red in autumn.

Country: Japan

MONKEY PUZZLE

The monkey puzzle doesn't look like any other tree. Its branches and trunk are covered in thick, spiky leaves. Its cones are long, brown and prickly.

Countries: Argentina and Chile

Living homes

Trees are living bug and animal homes! One oak tree can provide a home and food to hundreds of mammals, birds and insects. Oak trees also get lots of visitors during the day and at night time.

PIED FLYCATCHER

The pied flycatcher builds its nest in tree holes. The tree hole provides shelter, warmth and safety for the bird's young.

STAG BEETLE

Stag beetles get their name because their jaws look like a stag's antlers! Their larvae feed on rotten roots of trees underground.

FUNGUS

Fungi, such as mushrooms and toadstools, grow on or beneath oak trees. They get **nutrients** from the oak tree's roots.

ROOK

Rooks and other birds build their nests in the strong branches of oak trees. The nests are a safe place for the birds to lay their eggs. Pet cats and other predators can't reach the nests when they are so high above the ground.

CATERPILLAR

More minibeasts feed on oak trees than any other type of tree. Caterpillars eat oak tree leaves. This can sometimes damage the tree.

SQUIRREL

Squirrels bury acorns that they find beneath oak trees. They store the acorns for the winter. They also build their nests in the branches of oak trees.

DEER

Wherever there are oak trees, you are likely to see deer! Deer love to eat acorns. They forage beneath the oak tree, looking for acorns that have dropped to the floor.

BAT

Bats move into empty tree holes in the oak tree's trunk. This shelters them from the wind and rain.

Trees and us

Whether they are big, small, **deciduous** or **evergreen**, trees can be useful for people, animals and the environment.

FUEL

Fuel is any material that is burned to make heat or power. People have burned wood to make fire for millions of years.

FOOD

People and animals eat fruit, such as apples, cherries and plums, from trees. Nuts, such as hazelnuts, also grow on trees.

PAPER

It's hard to imagine a tall, strong tree being turned into small, weak sheets of paper. But that is exactly how paper is made! Wood from a tree is turned into pulp (a watery, woody soup). The pulp is dried and flattened into a long piece of paper. This is then cut into smaller sheets.

TIMBER

Timber is wood used for building useful things, such as houses, boats and furniture. Scots **pine** trunks are also used to build tall telephone poles.

MUSICAL INSTRUMENTS

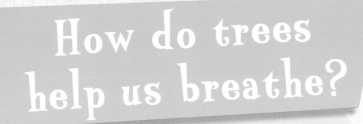

Wood is used to make all sorts of musical instruments, from pianos to xylophones. Guitars are usually made from mahogany, maple or sycamore. Violins are made from many different types of wood. The back, head and neck can be made from maple, the body from spruce and the chinrest from ebony!

TANNIN

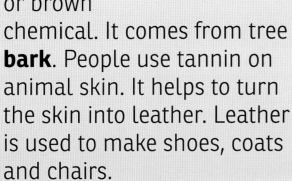

Tannin is a yellow or brown chemical. It comes from tree **bark**. People use tannin on animal skin. It helps to turn the skin into leather. Leather is used to make shoes, coats and chairs.

How do trees help us breathe?

Oxygen is a gas in the air. People and animals breathe in oxygen and breathe out **carbon dioxide**. Trees do the opposite during the day – they breathe out oxygen and breathe in carbon dioxide. Without trees, we would not survive.

CLEAN AIR

Trees can absorb and break down toxic (poisonous) gases from the air. This can help to keep the air clean and people healthier.

Glossary

bark outside cover of the trunk, branches and roots of a tree

carbon dioxide gas in the air that is needed by trees

cone seed of a pine tree

deciduous type of tree that loses its leaves once a year

evergreen type of tree with leaves that stay green all year round

forest large group of trees

husk outer covering of some seeds and fruits

nutrient food that helps the tree or plant to grow

orchard land planted with fruit or nut trees

oxygen gas in the air needed by humans and animals

photosynthesis way that trees and other plants use carbon dioxide, water and energy from the sun to make food

pine trees that have cones. Cones are the tree's seeds.

pollen fine yellow powder made by flowering trees and plants

pollination move or carry pollen from one flower to another. After pollination happens, seeds start to form.

sap liquid inside a tree. It carries nutrients and water to all parts of the tree

seed small part of a tree that can grow into a new tree

seedling very young tree or plant

shrub plant with woody stems

stately home large, old house that people can pay to visit

timber wood from trees used in some buildings

tree surgeon person who trims old or damaged trees to keep them healthy

Find out more

BOOKS

British Trees (Nature Detective), Victoria Munson (Wayland, 2016)

RSPB First Book of Trees, Derek Niemann (A & C Black Childrens & Educational, 2012)

Trees (What on Earth?), Kevin Warwick (QED Publishing, 2018)

WEBSITES

www.forestry.gov.uk/visit
Find a local wood or forest to visit at the Forestry Commission's website.

www.woodlandtrust.org.uk/naturedetectives/activities/2017/10/autumn-leaf-identification/
Ask your parents to help you download this worksheet. It will help you to identify different types of tree leaves.

Index